MELISSA BUBNIC is a playwright and screenwriter from Melbourne, currently living in London. She is a recipient of commissions and prizes from Arts Victoria, Ian Potter Cultural Trust, La Mama, Transport Accident Commission's 'Make a Film, Make a Difference' competition, Platform Youth Theatre and the Children's Literature Board of Australia. Her play *Stop. Rewind.* (dir. Anne Browning) premiered at Red Stitch Actors Theatre in Melbourne in 2010 and is touring nationally in 2012.

In 2011 Melissa completed a Masters in Writing for Performance at Goldsmiths, University of London with the assistance of the Rae and Edith Bennett Travelling Scholarship. Her play *Beached* won the 2010 Patrick White Award from the Sydney Theatre Company. Her latest play, *Emoticon*, was a winner of the Write Now 3 competition at the Brockley Jack Studio in London. Melissa is currently developing numerous TV projects, including an original comedy-drama series with Clerkenwell Films for Channel 4 (UK). She also writes for UK TV show, *Shameless*.

Giordano Gangl as Trevor, Olga Makeeva (seated) as Nina and Andrea Swifte as Heather in the 2010 production at Red Stitch Actors Theatre in Melbourne. (Photo: Jodie Hutchinson)

Melissa Bubnic

CURRENCY PLAYS

First published in 2012
by Currency Press Pty Ltd,
PO Box 2287, Strawberry Hills, NSW, 2012, Australia
enquiries@currency.com.au
www.currency.com.au

NATIONAL LIBRARY OF AUSTRALIA CIP DATA

Author:	Bubnic, Melissa.
Title:	Stop. rewind. / Melissa Bubnic.
ISBN:	9780868199504 (pbk.)
Dewey Number:	A822.4

Typeset by Dean Nottle for Currency Press.
Printed by Hyde Park Press, Richmond, SA.
Cover design by Katy Wall for Currency Press.

Stop. Rewind. was created with assistance from the Commonwealth Government through the Australia Council, its arts funding and advisory body.

Contents

Cover shows (from left) Andrea Swifte as Heather, Ian Rooney as Lachlan, Giordano Gangl as Trevor, Ella Caldwell as Tabitha, Tim Potter as Dim and Olga Makeeva as Nina in the 2010 production at Red Stitch Actors Theatre in Melbourne. (Photo: Gemma Higgins-Sears).

For Gerry
and everyone who changes us and never knows it.

INTRODUCTION

I was, in a word, depressed.

I had finished film school where I made two very shit short films that confirmed my total lack of genius. I was back working at the lowest rung in a large public sector bureaucracy, which had employed me on and off for the last six years. I spent my days alphabetising and filing forms that no-one would ever look at again, and listening to colleagues' anecdotes about their cats. I trawled through Wikipedia entries on famous despots (both of Slobodan Milosevic's parents committed suicide; Pol Pot's sister was the King's concubine; the evidence that Hitler had only one ball was shaky at best).

I couldn't sleep. Between all the reading on genocide, the YouTube mash-ups of animals attacking humans, and arrows pointing out the coke up a blurred, long-lens photo of Kate Moss's nose, I felt overwhelmingly anxious about the pointlessness of life. I found myself fantasising about contracting cancer, not something serious enough to kill me, just malignant enough so that death wasn't entirely ruled out and then I could overcome it—with grace and dignity of course—and the experience would transform me somehow, give me purpose, help me appreciate the gift of life which I had hitherto been wasting.

I expressed my anxiety about the meaninglessness of life to a colleague. She was in her mid-forties, a chronic smoker, and had a wit so dry you could stick an olive in her and call it a martini. She clucked sympathetically and reassured me that no-one's life had any meaning, there was no point to anything, and that I would be far happier to embrace nihilism and thereby remain sane… and employed. And then she popped out for a fag, grimly cheerful in the certainty of her death from tobacco-related disease.

I've thought a lot about that conversation since, and what it says about class and a generational shift in expectations. My parents couldn't understand my moaning either. I had a life they could never have hoped for themselves—education, no responsibilities, independence. And I was still in the dumps.

Both of my parents started their working life young. At age fourteen, my mother entered the factory where she cut threads and checked buttonholes on men's shorts; at age fifteen, my father became an apprentice plumber at Gas and Fuel. To them, a job was not a life calling; it did not define you. The point of employment was to work, to earn, to buy, and to live. That was all well and good for people like my parents—migrants, salt-of-the-earth folk, the sort of people Gauguin would've painted, for whom, honest toil was satisfying in and of itself. (Obviously, I'm being a bit of a dick but you get my drift…)

But me? I'm different. I'm 'special'. I'm part of a narcissistic generation for whom existential fulfilment is not only an expectation, but a serious life imperative. Maybe it's the rise of self-help culture which promises personal satisfaction in eight easy steps, or the predominance of reality TV shows that promise wholesale transformation—but somewhere along the line, I got this crazy idea that I was supposed to enjoy my job, that it said something fundamental about who I was and the kind of life I wanted to live. As my parents rightly suspected, university had ruined me, given me airs, filled my head full of bullshit and completely screwed up my priorities.

The problem, I think, is that for most of my life I've lived with two versions of myself—maybe many of us do. There's the self that is (you know, clumsy, half-formed, farts when I think no-one can pin it on me), and the self I would like to become that's forever out of reach (confident, immensely successful, surrounded by cool friends and loved ones and awards and a fridge that makes ice cubes). Perhaps the thing about growing up is that the self you wish you were starts to seem less important than just enjoying yourself now. No-one knows what the future will bring or when it'll bring it. Heartbreak? Disease? Senility? Death? If I'm going to be hit by a bus tomorrow in underwear my mother wouldn't approve of, no point in holding back on the cheesecake today.

Seizing life by the balls (or 'the bull by the undies', as Heather would say) is something I've thought about a lot. A week shy of his fiftieth birthday, a senior colleague, Gerry, was diagnosed with pancreatic cancer and given a month to live. I didn't know this man well. We'd exchange grimaces that would pass for smiles when we'd cross paths in the hallway. We'd comment on weather, or the dwindling milk supply as we shuffled around each other making tea in the staff kitchen. I think he was rather shy but I never made much of an effort to find out.

We sent him a get-well-soon card and flowers. We wrote horribly inadequate messages like, 'Hope you feel better', 'Can't wait to see you back on your feet'. We tut-tutted the terrible shame of it all. He'd done everything right. Lived within his means. Paid off his mortgage. People who knew him well and for a long time spoke of the romance he might have had if only he'd had the courage to act. They spoke of his retirement plans, how he was going to travel the world. We'd look down at our shoes, shake our heads, wipe tears from our eyes. It was just so… so bloody unfair. And you could see it, the panic, the dawning realisation in all of us that this could happen to me too. At any moment I could die and I'm not ready, I'm not ready at all and I haven't done the things I wanted to do, or said the things I wanted to say, and I haven't even worked out what the hell those things are anyway.

None of us can know how we're going to feel at the end, or if we will have time to feel anything at all. Someone once told me that unfulfilled dreams are less scary than you think. Think of all that energy and anxiety spent chasing something, wanting something, needing something… and then one day you realise, you know, you really know that it's not going to happen. You're not going to leave your wife, you're never going to play Hamlet, your son isn't going to forgive you. You might be broken by it… or actually relieved. Because now you can let it go. This terrible weight of failure, this unbearable sadness, a noose around your neck, and finally you can let it go. But maybe it's only in trying and failing that you can let it go. Maybe the things we don't try for stay with us a lot longer.

According to Bronnie Ware, a nurse who spent several years working in palliative care, the most common regret of the dying is… 'I wish I'd had the courage to live a life true to myself, not the life others expected of me'. It's pretty bloody hard to live life on your own terms. Maybe impending death clarifies things, and you can look back on your life and see how it was all a series of choices, and the reasons that motivated you to make one choice over another don't seem to resonate so much anymore. But from this side of things, where the future is unknown terrain, and you have to make your path, it doesn't always feel like we have choices. There are bills to pay, and kids to provide for, and parents to support, and you can't just take risks because people could get hurt, you could be letting them down, or it might not work out the way you hope anyway, and you can't just change your life… can you?

I know one person who did. Another colleague and friend who inspired the character of Trevor (not his real name) was profoundly affected by Gerry's death. Trevor always dreamed of going to Europe. He got close once. He booked the flights, packed his bags. He actually even made it to the airport before the panic attack overwhelmed him and he returned home, full of self-loathing and a deep, abiding depression.

But Gerry's death made something switch over in Trevor and he didn't want it switched back. He got his first boyfriend. He went to Europe. He threw a fortieth birthday party where he invited friends and family. He made a speech about life being too short and to hell with fear and self-doubt. And then he sang 'Leaving on a Jet Plane'. Everyone in that room knew that they were witnessing something special, that this was transformation, this was courage. For an evening, I think we felt a tremendous sense of optimism, like anything and everything was possible.

Melissa Bubnic
London, May 2012

Stop. Rewind. was first produced by Red Stitch Actors Theatre at East St Kilda on 21 July 2010 with the following cast:

NINA	Olga Makeeva
HEATHER	Andrea Swifte
TABITHA	Ella Caldwell
GRANT / RENE	James Taylor
DIM (DEMETRIOS)	Tim Potter
TREVOR	Giordano Gangl
LACHLAN / RICHARD	Ian Rooney

Director, Anne Browning
Designer, Peter Mumford
Lighting Designer, Stelios Karagiannis
Production Manager, Linda Hum

Stop. Rewind. was developed in conjunction with Red Stitch Actors Theatre.

CHARACTERS

NINA, a Ukrainian in her late thirties
HEATHER, fifty-seven years old
TABITHA, thirty-three years old
GRANT, forty-three years old
DIM (DEMITRIOS), twenty-five years old
TREVOR, forty-eight years old but feels fifty
LACHLAN, in his fifties
RENE, Nina's French husband, forty-one years old
PHONE OPERATOR, any gender or age
RICHARD, sixty-one years old
CHORUS, a role to be shared by the ensemble of performers

This play is to be performed by seven actors. The performer who plays Lachlan could also play Richard. The performer who plays Grant could also play Rene.

SET DESIGN

The majority of the action takes place in an open-plan government department office. Each character has a cubicle. The idea of individual cubicles is suggested not through walls but by the way they own their individual space. When characters are in the office, they do not walk but glide along a series of conveyer systems in the same automated way that goods travel through the factory process.

A NOTE ON THE TEXT

A new line indicates that a new Chorus member should begin speaking.

A line with no full stop at the end of a speech indicates that the next speech follows on immediately.

The use of '/' marks the point that the next line should begin.

SCENE ONE

The office. The production line.

TABITHA *opens letters with a letter opener and retrieves the document inside. She hands the document to* HEATHER.

HEATHER *unfolds the document and stamps it. She hands the document to* NINA.

NINA *signs the document. She hands the document to* DIM.

DIM *hole-punches the document. He hands the document to* GRANT.

GRANT *refolds the document and hands it back to* DIM.

DIM *passes the document back up the chain.*

TREVOR *enters the scene. He travels along the conveyer system towards his desk.*

CHORUS: THE MONDAY.

Perhaps if you had an acquired brain injury
Or some other reason for not knowing the day of the week
This statement may be helpful…

HEATHER: Another Monday, eh Trevor?

CHORUS: Heather is currently rehearsing her Lady Bracknell for the Strathmore Theatrical Arts Group production of *The Importance of Being Earnest*.

HEATHER: [*with Received Pronunciation accent*] Another Monday, eh love?

CHORUS: If Trevor had any courage he would have liked to

TREVOR *smacks* HEATHER *in the face with his keyboard.*

But Trevor wasn't courageous
So instead he said

TREVOR: Yes.

HEATHER: Everything alright, love?

CHORUS: This wasn't a question.

This was manners where you ask someone how they are and they say

Fine

Rather than the truth which could be very unpleasant like

TREVOR: I've got a fungal infection on the head of my penis and it's getting me a bit down.

HEATHER: Everything alright, love?

TREVOR: Yes.

HEATHER: Did I tell you about Patrick and Anna, love?

CHORUS: Heather wrote a poem for Patrick and Anna's wedding.

The poem had actions.

TREVOR: Um… new carpet?

HEATHER: They had an ice-cream. At Harrods.

She laughs.

CHORUS: Trevor thought Heather was missing a piece of her frontal lobe.

TREVOR: Oh.

TREVOR *sits and joins in the production line. He shreds each document he receives without looking at it.*

HEATHER: Another Monday, eh Nina? Tabitha?

She laughs.

NINA: Always Heather.

CHORUS: Nina doesn't know that her colleagues call her Stalin because she's Ukrainian and a ballbreaker.

Stalin was Georgian.

It's all East—bad hair and synthetic pants.

TABITHA: You can't stop the Mondays.

CHORUS: Tabitha loves planning holidays in rural Victoria.

She sends postcards to colleagues 'wishing they could smell the clean country air too'

And then forces them to thumb through her five hundred photos of a disused mill in Edithvale.

HEATHER: Did I tell you that Patrick and Anna had an ice-cream—at *Harrods?* In *England?*

CHORUS: There was no-one Heather hadn't told.

HEATHER: Don't tell me you tipped Richmond, Dim?

DIM: Someone's got to keep the Tiger fires burning, fine lady.

CHORUS: Dim plays lead guitar in his band, Roy 23.

This gig in admin is just temporary

Only he's been doing it for thirteen months now.

HEATHER: Good morning, Grant.

CHORUS: Grant started working for the DDDPTS when it was still just the DDD back in 1989.

He likes Aussie films. He hates Tom Hanks.

GRANT: Seven from eight. If fricken Collingwood knew what a bloody football looked like I would've had a clean sweep!

LACHLAN *enters. He walks (he does not use the conveyer system) to Sammy's desk.*

Careful, serfs—here comes his lordship.

HEATHER: Good morning, Lachlan.

CHORUS: Lachlan moved from Sydney one and a half years ago to become GM of the department.

He is trying to remember something about AFL that he saw in the news. (Who was it that stuffed his groin?)

So he can appear relatable to these arseholes on Level Seven.

HEATHER: Did you get my email about [*adopting a RP accent*] *Ernest,* or *The Importance Thereof?*

CHORUS: Lachlan would rather suckle horse testicles than go to an amateur theatre production in Strathmore.

LACHLAN: Another Monday, eh? At least we're all in it together.

GRANT: Except some of us are well in the shit and others just get the occasional waft from the top.

CHORUS: If Lachlan was less mature

(And more clever)

He would call Grant… some pun on shit that would cut Grant in two, the useless cunt.

LACHLAN: Good morning, Grant. Demitrios.

CHORUS: Instead

He plans to wipe snot on Grant's desk before leaving.

GRANT: To what do we plebs owe the pleasure?

LACHLAN: Sam not in yet?

Everyone looks to Sammy's empty cubicle.

GRANT: He alleges he can't shake this stomach thing. Lazy sod.

GRANT *turns another page of the newspaper.*

LACHLAN *stares at him.*

LACHLAN: Well… don't break your back with effort.

LACHLAN *picks his nose and wipes it on Grant's desk unseen.*

He leaves.

HEATHER: How was your weekend, love?

From left: Andrea Swifte as Heather, Tim Potter as Dim, Olga Makeeva as Nina, Ian Rooney (standing) as Lachlan, Ella Caldwell as Tabitha and Giordano Gangl as Trevor in the 2010 production at Red Stitch Actors Theatre in Melbourne. (Photo: Gemma Higgins-Sears)

Everything stops.

Everyone faces the audience.

EVERYONE: [*in unison*] Good.

Beat.

Great.

Beat.

Okay.

NINA: Meh…

TABITHA: I stripped back the skirting boards. I'll be dead before that house is finished but everyone needs a hobby.

DIM: Just went out with some mates. Few drinks. Nothing scandalous.

LACHLAN *re-enters.*

LACHLAN: I—

CHORUS: No-one asks Lachlan about his weekend.

LACHLAN: Oh.

LACHLAN *leaves.*

NINA: I made a soup will last a month. I freeze it. You go home you have borscht. Ready.

GRANT: The usual. Hector's footy Saturday. Charlotte's basketball Sunday.

HEATHER: I played tennis Saturday morning and had lunch with friends—I just had a salad but they put pine nuts in which I thought was nice—you never saw pine nuts anywhere ten years ago. And then I saw a movie Saturday night with my sister and her neighbour—some awful thing with Sandra Bullock—don't any of these women eat? We had a coffee afterwards which I shouldn't have done because I don't normally drink coffee so late and it was a nuisance because I took ages to get to sleep and I had to get up early Sunday because I wanted to clean the shower and bake a lemon slice because Virginia was coming round with the kids. So I really didn't have a minute to myself—it was all so rush rush.

TREVOR *gives a long sigh.*

CHORUS: This is what they don't tell you about their weekend…

DIM: I snorted a shitload of speed and fingered an anorexic chick hoping for more from both.

TABITHA: My mother hit me when I tried to make her shower. She hates the shower. She lies and says she's already washed. But this time I smacked her back and screamed. No words. Just… scream.

HEATHER: Virginia didn't come. Molly had an ear infection.

GRANT: I spent most of Saturday arvo in the shed. Drinking beer and listening to the Tigers lose. I hid the cans in next-door's rubbish. I think Rachel hates me.

NINA: Rene didn't even look at me. Not once.

TREVOR *gives a long sigh.*

HEATHER: What a shame the weekend ends so soon. Yes, another Monday. Oh well. Tomorrow will be Tuesday and then Wednesday and before you know it it'll be Friday and then the weekend and we'll be doing it all over again.

TREVOR *vomits into his paper bin.*

SCENE TWO

The office.

Everyone stands in their cubicle, facing the audience. The phone on Sammy's desk rings.

CHORUS: THE GET-WELL-SOON CARD.

A week shy of his fiftieth birthday

Sammy saw the doctor about that stomach ache.

NINA: Dear Sam…

LACHLAN: On behalf of us all here…

CHORUS: Sammy started working for the department when he still had a full head of hair.

TREVOR: Get well soon.

CHORUS: And now he's the Deputy Manager.

And bald.

DIM: Grant's running amok!

CHORUS: The doctor did tests.

DIM: I've had to pull him into line with a few loose elbows.

CHORUS: Sammy has been meaning to take sailing lessons for the past several years.

He subscribes to *Sailing Breezes Magazine*. He has a sailor's cap—

You know, like the one the captain wears in *Gilligan's Island*? Some evenings he wears it while watching television.

GRANT: Arrow pointing to Dim's message. Dim hasn't even showed up since you've been away!

CHORUS: The doctor booked Sammy in to see an oncologist later that week.

HEATHER: We miss you very much. God love and keep you.

CHORUS: Sammy was in love once.

With a lady no-one thought too bright but he loved the way she sneezed tiny little sneezes always in a sequence of three and he thought her overbite was sexier than Rita Hayworth's.

But he never told her that he loved her.

She ended up marrying a methadone addict who stole her car when he left twenty years later.

NINA: Thinking of you at this difficult time.

CHORUS: Sammy was hoping for an operable cyst.

But instead he was told…

TABITHA: I'm saving that bottle of pinot grigio for when you come back to work.

CHORUS: That he had pancreatic cancer.

And had a month to live.

LACHLAN: You take as much time as you need. Look forward to having you back as good as new.

CHORUS: His favourite film is *When Harry Met Sally*

But he tells people it's *Breaker Morant.*

Sammy's phone continues to ring.

SCENE THREE

Tabitha's bedroom.

GRANT *and* TABITHA *are lying in Tabitha's bed.*

GRANT: You know he just paid off that mortgage? He would've been better off spending it on heroin and whores.

TABITHA: I don't want to talk about it.

TABITHA'S MUM: [*offstage*] Tabitha!

TABITHA: It's just the radio, Mum!

TABITHA *turns on the radio.*

GRANT: What's the reward? Cancer and the satisfaction of being debt-free.

TABITHA: I said I don't want to talk about it!

TABITHA'S MUM: [*offstage*] Tabitha!

TABITHA: THE RADIO! THE RADIO!

TABITHA *lights a cigarette.*

GRANT: It gets you thinking—

TABITHA: I don't want to think.

GRANT: It's got me thinking, Tabby, I want—

CHORUS: Grant wants to tell Tabitha that he's been hiding money from his wife in an old pair of Explorer socks so he and Tabitha can afford a place of their own.

Twenty from the shopping here.

A hundred and seventy-three from a pokies win there.

He's looking at two-bedroom rental properties because he wants her mother to come live with them too because he really loves her—

Tabitha—

Not so much her mum who he's never met because Tabitha makes him sneak in through the back while she distracts her mum in the front.

Instead he says

GRANT: I wish… you'd stop smoking.

TABITHA: Why? So I can die of something else?

GRANT: That's the classic smoker's excuse, isn't it? We all gotta die of something so why not emphysema. What's a few gangrenous toes?

TABITHA: I've been smoking my entire life. Cigarettes will kill me. I accept that.

GRANT: Nothing's certain. A year ago we didn't know this would happen.

Beat.

TABITHA: No.

GRANT: You should stop smoking.

TABITHA: There's a lot of things we should stop but we don't, do we?

Beat.

GRANT: Tabby, this isn't… some nasty little affair, you know? I really care about you. I'm not the same person I was… because of you.

CHORUS: Grant can't believe how shit he sounds. He's rehearsed this speech a thousand times and now he sounds like a song even Bryan Adams would be too embarrassed to record.

TABITHA: Grant, don't be daft!

GRANT: I know the circumstances are less than ideal…

CHORUS: And now he sounds like a mortgage manager!

GRANT: But this is the best thing that's ever happened to me.

TABITHA: Grant, I'm not proud of this. I'm not proud of fucking the middle-aged guy from work before he goes home to dinner with his family—'after peak hour'—and I heat up a Lean Cuisine and watch 'Border Security' with my demented mother.

GRANT: What are you so afraid of?

TABITHA: You have this ridiculous idea that this is some 1940s melodrama and I'm Bette Davis and you're Paul Henreid—'let's don't ask for the moon, we got the stars'.

CHORUS: Black-and-white—

Of course.

Tracking in for the close-up.

Glistening eyes and trembling hands.

Can't hold her cigarette steady.

TABITHA: I know why you have to see it like that—but I can't. I'm sorry I just can't play along. This is Moonee Ponds and my bedspread's from Target and all of this is so… ordinary.

CHORUS: The only way to deal with a feisty dame is to seize her.

Kiss her savagely.

GRANT: I saw myself more as Joseph Cotten. Thought Henreid was a bit… you know.

GRANT *makes a limp-wrist motion.*

TABITHA: He wasn't gay, Grant.

CHORUS: She slaps you.

'So you wanna play rough, do ya?'

Kiss her again. Harder.

GRANT: Prefer Cotten. More masculine.

TABITHA: Fine. Be Joseph Cotten.

CHORUS: She yields.

GRANT: Are you happy as Bette Davis?

TABITHA: I said I wasn't playing.

CHORUS: Music swells.

And you're Bogart and Bacall!

You're Hepburn and Tracy!

You're—

GRANT: No. You're better as you. Tabby Cat. Femme fatale. With cigarettes and scotch on ice. She's never ordinary.

CHORUS: Iris on you and her and the rest of the world ain't worth a damn.

GRANT *makes a miaow sound.*

TABITHA'S MUM: [*offstage*] Tabitha!

TABITHA: [*to* GRANT] She's locked herself in the fucking loo again. [*Calling out*] The latch is on the door, Mum! You have to jiggle the latch!

TABITHA'S MUM: [*offstage*] Tabitha!

TABITHA: The latch!

GRANT: Tabby—

TABITHA: Don't 'Tabby' me, Grant—

GRANT: I can't stop thinking—

TABITHA'S MUM: [*offstage*] Tabitha!

TABITHA: JUST JIGGLE THE FUCKING LATCH!

GRANT: I love you.

Beat.

TABITHA: I—

GRANT: I love you.

Pause.

TABITHA: I've got to get Mum off the toilet.

TABITHA *leaves.*

GRANT *stares after her.*

CHORUS: What Grant wanted to say was

GRANT: You don't get a warning. Just the death sentence and no bloody time to put things right. And if I'm gonna die tomorrow—I'd rather have given it a go. With you. And if I lose—so what? I'm losing now anyway. And once you're already losing—fuck the score. This is our chance. Don't you see that?

CHORUS: But Grant didn't know how to say that. And he was scared of what she'd say if he did.

So instead he said

To no-one in particular

GRANT: I like the bedspread.

SCENE FOUR

The office.

Everyone stands facing the audience.

NINA, HEATHER, TABITHA, GRANT *and* DIM *are passing large cards to each other. Each card has a few letters printed on it. They are attempting to arrange the cards so that the message reads, from left to right, 'HAPPY BIRTHDAY TREVOR'. This task is impossible.*

CHORUS: THE BIRTHDAY.

On his forty-eight birthday Trevor gets to work forty three minutes late. In the early days

Trevor would've offered an overcooked excuse for his lateness.

Something like…

TREVOR: Heart attack. On the Belgrave line. A man could be dead by the time you wait for an ambulance in this city…

CHORUS: Or…

TREVOR: She just fell. I actually heard the hip snap. Like a bread stick. An old woman could be dead by the time you wait for an ambulance in this city…

CHORUS: But today

He regrets getting to work at all.

Beat.

TREVOR: I'm going to the loo.

HEATHER *hands* TREVOR *a party hat, which he reluctantly puts on.*

CHORUS: And there he spends an hour and seventeen minutes regretting everything

Every decision he's ever made

Because it brought him to this point.

Alone.

In the men's toilets.

At age forty-eight.

The only thing to mark this dubious occasion is thirty minutes in the tearoom.

Some awful Safeway four-dollar cake.

Warm juice. Painful conversations about the weather

And whichever pensioner has recently been bashed by disenfranchised youth on the way to get their arthritis medication.

Lots of—

TABITHA: That's right.

CHORUS: And

HEATHER: [*laughing*] Absolutely.

Everyone sings 'Happy Birthday'.

HEATHER *gives her performance the full mezzo-soprano treatment.*

TABITHA: [*holding one lit birthday candle*] Dear Trevor. I hope you have a great birthday. Best wishes. Tabitha.

HEATHER: Wishing you all the best on your special day. Heather.

DIM: [*throwing one streamer*] Big Man Bombasero. Save me some cake. Dim.

CHORUS: Always the same two men fighting over who says the—

DIM & GRANT: Hip-hip!

CHORUS: To the crowd's

EVERYONE: Hoo-ray!

CHORUS: Last night Trevor called a helpline…

TREVOR: What's the point? I know how it's going to end.

PHONE OPERATOR: Trevor, I've told you. This helpline is for children in distress. This is the third time tonight you've called.

TREVOR: And that depresses me.

PHONE OPERATOR: Trevor, this is an emergency service.

TREVOR: This is an emergency. I'm hovering in nothingness here!

PHONE OPERATOR: We've referred you to a counselling service for ongoing help. I'm sorry but we're not the best people to help you.

TREVOR: I'm forty-eight years old and I haven't done a thing. Do you understand? It's not that I've got so much left to do—it's that I've got everything left to do because I haven't done anything.

PHONE OPERATOR: I'm sorry, Trevor. I want to help—I really do.

TREVOR: And I'm not going to do any of it, am I? Because I'll still be me.

PHONE OPERATOR: This service is for children who need immediate intervention.

TREVOR: Everything I've ever done is wrong.

PHONE OPERATOR: While we're on the phone with you some teenager is about to throw himself off the West Gate because he keeps getting the engaged signal. Please, Trevor—

TREVOR: I bought some rope today.

Beat.

PHONE OPERATOR: You bought rope?

TREVOR: I told Gonzalo—he's who served me, Latin-type, very good-looking—I wanted to make a tyre swing for my kid. He looked at me like he thought I was lying. I don't look like a man who has kids? Or I don't look like a man who'd make them a swing? Or I don't look like a man?

PHONE OPERATOR: These are your thoughts—not his.

TREVOR: He convinced me to buy nylon over the natural fibres. Said the lifespan of the rope—the nylon—was longer. I thought that funny—lifespan of the rope business—funny—given the circumstances.

PHONE OPERATOR: Are you going to make a tyre swing?

TREVOR: In the movies there's always a beam or something—a hook—but not in my flat. So now I have to go back to Gonzalo and buy a hook or bracket or something—something you can hang a rope off. And what would Gonzalo think then?

PHONE OPERATOR: He'd think you're a man who wants a bracket.

TREVOR: I sat down to write the letter. I thought about not leaving anything. Like that would be a grander statement.

PHONE OPERATOR: Trevor—

TREVOR: But then not leaving a note makes it look impulsive, like I hadn't thought it through.

CHORUS: Trevor thinks everything through.

He thinks the order in which his name appears in the address line of an email reveals how the sender ranks him.

TREVOR: I don't want to be trashy about it.

PHONE OPERATOR: You need help.

TREVOR: Tell me what you think about this first draft. I start with a quote from Sting—

PHONE OPERATOR: No, Trevor.

TREVOR: It's okay. It's from when he was with The Police.

PHONE OPERATOR: I mean I'm not listening to your letter. That's not what we do here. We don't advise on suicide notes.

TREVOR: I wouldn't be calling you if I had someone else to ask.

PHONE OPERATOR: You should be in therapy, Trevor. Please don't call here again.

TREVOR: I can't afford therapy! Even with the Medicare rebate I'm at least sixty bucks out of pocket!

PHONE OPERATOR *hangs up.*

TREVOR *hangs up.*

Beat.

He dials a number.

Hello? Is this for Parents Without Partners?

By the end of the scene, the cards do read from left to right: 'HAPPY BIRTHDAY TREVOR'.

DIM *blows a party whistle (the kind with a paper tube that unfurls when blown) in* TREVOR*'s face.*

SCENE FIVE

Rene and Nina's house.

NINA: No, Rene!

RENE: Fuck you, Ninotchka! You're not my boss!

NINA: Fuck me? Fuck you!

RENE: You have the brain of a peasant. No imagination, no vision—

NINA: You have the vision of a fucking idiot!

RENE: If Einstein showed you 'e equals mc squared' you would have sold the formula for two turnips and a potato and thought yourself rich.

NINA: You're not even a pimple on Einstein's arse, you fucking homo!

RENE: Homo?

NINA: You haven't touched me in a year.

RENE: I wish I was a homo. I could do with intellectual stimulation instead of talking to a goat!

Pause.

Ninotchka—

NINA: Rene, we might be able to keep the house. This is a blessing, this is our blessing—

RENE: Blessing? Cancer? A man will die, Ninotchka.

CHORUS: How long after hearing of Sammy's cancer did Nina think about taking his job?

Well, life does go on. Is that wrong?

It's not like she gave him the cancer.

NINA: I said our blessing, not his blessing. It's an extra twenty grand a year—it's our house. We can… we might still keep our house.

CHORUS: After years of being the bitch for saying no to the girls' demands for Bettina Liano jeans and Mac make-up and a Wii now that they're bored of the PlayStation they got second-hand from the Monterisos up the road

After years of that piece-of-shit 1990 Nissan Pulsar Vector that routinely refuses to go beyond third gear

After years of dreading admitting to her mother that she is a failure who can no longer afford to send money back to the Ukraine

After sleeplessness and the stress-induced ulcer and the ever-present immigrant fear of poverty

Nina feels now that she might just be able to breathe.

NINA: This is a gift.

RENE: Yes, our chance if we invest smart—

NINA: No! You promised me. No more get-rich-quick dreams. It was the only reason I let you come back—

RENE: This is different!

NINA: You promised proper job with proper pay. You promised. You're forty-one, Rene. You're a man, yes? Enough with the dreams. Enough.

RENE: You never listen! This is big idea—big. Two, three years we never work again—trust me.

NINA: First with the fruit—door-to-door fruit. Who doesn't want nectarines at their door fresh?

RENE: Name one person who doesn't!

NINA: Then the magnets.

RENE: That fucking Giorgio stole the product!

NINA: Because you went into business with a junkie!

RENE: Because he's a commerce genius!

NINA: But a junkie!

RENE: I tell you—someone is going to make a lot of money out of those magnets. The mattresses cure cancer.

NINA: The ostrich farm?

Beat.

RENE: Okay. I made mistakes there.

NINA: They died. Every fucking bird a fortune and they died.

RENE: Because I was cheap! Because I had you bleating in my ears about money, money, money, and I didn't get the immunisation done because you said we couldn't afford it!

NINA: We couldn't!

RENE: I listened to you—a peasant with no head for business.

NINA: Manuel says there's jobs at his factory.

Beat.

RENE: The pie factory? You want I should make pies? Stand all day like a machine and make pies?

NINA: You promised proper job with proper pay.

RENE: I read philosophy. I understand economics—

NINA: And you threw my money away on dead birds!

RENE: *Your* money?

NINA: It's been almost two years, Rene, you been made redundant.

RENE: I've worked—

NINA: At the club! You drink what you earn and then pay some more. Think of Sabi, Anna—don't they deserve a wedding? Or do they have to get married at McDonald's because their father was too proud to earn?

RENE: You want I should take a job where I get paid 30 per cent less what I used to make for some fucking 20-year-old to freeze my pay, tell me make sacrifice and he snort cocaine? I trained as a boilermaker. That's highly skilled work. There's no jobs for someone with the experience I got.

NINA: Fuck your experience! This is now. So you don't get paid what you think you deserve—the point is you get paid.

RENE: That's the problem with your whole fucking world. Everyone compromise. You get kicked in the face. They make you redundant. They steal your benefits for each other and you left with nothing and then what? You s'pose to beg their friend for a job to get paid less, to get kicked more? Or you go to the factory and forget the whole reason you became highly skilled is so you don't end up in the fucking factory with all the other robots!

Beat.

I'm not a nothing. I won't give up and be a nothing. A fucking little squeak in the wheels.

NINA: Everyone starts at the beginning. If you're smart, if you work hard—you don't stay on the floor forever. I come with no English. And now I'm the boss.

RENE: This bloody world you live in. One man's cancer is your immigrant dream.

NINA: Now the failed capitalist grows a conscience? Go pull your dick in the toilet, Rene—not with me.

RENE: How excited you must've been, Ninotchka—when you heard yes? Cancer? One month to go? Where's the champagne? Praise to God for the rotten pancreas! Now it's your turn to be the parasite in middle management to administer parking fines and dog shit.

Beat.

CHORUS: If Nina could sift through the rage and disgust and hatred she feels for her husband right now she'd find this

NINA: I love you, Rene. I love that you still think you understand Heidegger—you don't. I know how important it is to you to be important. I know how you saw it in your head—an empire, a fortune, you a king. But, Rene, you are not a king. You could still become a man.

CHORUS: But Nina can't sift through her rage and disgust and hatred because she is not a sieve

And emotions don't come apart as easy as flour.

So instead she says

NINA: Get the fuck out of my house before I cut off your balls.

SCENE SIX

The office.

Everyone sits in their cubicle.

Everyone is focused on their computer screens.

NINA *is at Sammy's desk, removing his items and placing them in a box marked 'Sammy's things'. She is putting up her things in their stead.*

CHORUS: TIME THEFT.

Time theft is when employees 'steal' from their employers by wilfully wasting time for which they are being paid.

If you're watching a waterskiing squirrel on YouTube—

HEATHER *laughs at her screen, delighted.*

HEATHER: That's so cute!

TABITHA: Show me! Show me!

CHORUS: When you're supposed to be working—

That's time theft.

TABITHA: Ooh! He's wearing a little ski vest!

CHORUS: If you're playing some reaction game where you have to click the mouse before the sheep bolt out of the paddock—

DIM *and* GRANT *furiously click their mice.*

DIM & GRANT: Fuck!

CHORUS: That's time theft.

NINA: I know none of you are working but you could give me the fucking respect to pretend. My eyes work—I'm not Sammy.

GRANT: She just sits in his chair.

NINA: What?

The rest of the scene is composed mostly of emails (except for NINA*'s dialogue). At the end of each email, we hear the 'email sent' and 'email arrived' sounds.*

CHORUS: Trevor is writing an email to Dim…

TREVOR: I don't feel there are a lot of people I can talk to. I really value our friendship. I really do. I—

TREVOR *looks around to ensure no-one is 'listening' in.*

He lowers his voice.

I don't know if you know but I'm actually gay. Did you know? Is it really obvious?

DIM: No, it's not… obvious. I just thought it was possible. You know… because you're intelligent and like art-house cinema.

TREVOR: I'm not—

He looks around to ensure no-one is listening in.

He lowers his voice.

I'm not in the closet but I… if it's okay, I'd prefer that you don't mention it to anyone.

DIM: Of course.

CHORUS: Dim is writing an email to Grant…

DIM: Big Trev just fessed he likes sausage! Lol.

TREVOR: It's just… you know Heather's so conservative. And Catholic.

CHORUS: Grant responds to Dim's email…

GRANT: Really? What next? Heather's an old gasbag and Nina used to manage a gulag?

CHORUS: Grant writes an email to Tabitha…

GRANT: Trev just told Dim he's gay and has sworn him to secrecy. He thought no-one knew! Surprised emoticon. X. X.

CHORUS: Tabitha responds to Grant's email…

TABITHA: Are you twelve? And please keep your emails professional. Delete correspondence from inbox, outbox and trash.

CHORUS: Tabitha writes an email to Heather…

TABITHA: Trevor thought no-one knew he was gay. Exclamation mark.

CHORUS: Heather responds to Tabitha's email…

HEATHER: I thought everyone knew he was a little queer? You can tell by how he walks.

CHORUS: Trevor sends an email to Dim…

TREVOR: I just wanted to—

He looks around to ensure no-one is listening.

He lowers his voice.

—tell you I'm gay and… I've met someone.

Beat.

A man.

Beat.

A lover.

CHORUS: Dim is writing an email to Grant…

DIM: Trev's having sex with a man! He actually called him 'a lover'! I'm so happy I didn't call in sick today! Seventeen exclamation marks. Happy face emoticon.

The email is forwarded on to each other team member. The sounds of emails being sent and received. Everyone laughs in turn.

TREVOR *looks around suspiciously.*

NINA: What? Again with the squirrel on the skis?

CHORUS: Dim writes an email to Trevor…

DIM: You sly dog. The Big Bomb's greasing up!

TREVOR: I know you're going to hate this but he is a really good guy but he's a… parking inspector. I know that's awful.

DIM: Who cares about his job?

TREVOR: I know I'm no prize. It's been long enough between drinks to do some good thinking and I know that I'm… you know, no prize. Aesthetically.

DIM: Trevor, there's nothing wrong with you.

CHORUS: Dim was lying.

TREVOR: There's another thing. His name is… Trevor.

Beat.

DIM *types furiously. The sounds of emails being sent and received. Everyone laughs in turn.*

NINA: What? Now a moose wears a panama hat? A cat in a blender? What?

Everyone focuses on their screens.

TREVOR: It's weird, isn't it? Trevor and Trevor?

CHORUS: Dim wondered if Trevor—

Not this Trevor—

The other Trevor—

Was actually real and Trevor—

This Trevor—

Lacked the most basic capacity for imagination that he couldn't think of any other name to give this fictional boyfriend but his own.

DIM: It's a little weird but honestly, Trevor, who cares? As long as he's a good guy…

TREVOR: We were getting along so well—I couldn't believe it. I actually thought… maybe I've been wrong all this time. Maybe this could happen for me—it's happening! I'm just like everybody else! And then… we were in bed the other morning and he said… (please keep this confidential) he said… he wanted me to turn over, to lie on my back and he would… he would—

Beat.

He wants to wax my balls.

Beat.

Don't you think that's appallingly rude?

DIM: I haven't seen your balls but you are a bit of a gorilla, mate.

TREVOR: My balls aren't the problem!

DIM: Clearly they are.

TREVOR: If he wants some waxed teenager in stovepipe jeans go to The Market! He doesn't like *me!* The real me! I called a helpline that specialises in abusive relationships—you can't be too careful. He could be a complete nut job wanting to flambé my penis! I had to break up with him. I just didn't feel safe. He's very built.

DIM *types an email. The sound of emails arriving in each team member's inbox.*

GRANT: I told you he's half-mongoloid.

TABITHA: He's allergic to happiness.

HEATHER *hovers at* TREVOR*'s desk until he looks up.*

She puts a hand on his shoulder.

HEATHER: Have a biscuit, love.

CHORUS: Trevor sends Dim an email…

TREVOR: I'm fifty.

DIM: No you're not. You're forty-eight.

TREVOR: What's the difference?

DIM: Two years.

TREVOR: I'm fifty and I've wasted my life. I couldn't change now even if I wanted to.

DIM: Why?

TREVOR: I don't know how to be anyone else. They're going to get rid of me, Dim.

DIM: Bullshit! Why? What have you heard?

CHORUS: Everyone knew that they—being Stalin and management—were trying to get rid of Trevor.

TREVOR: I've gone too far. I've become too complacent.

CHORUS: Dim thought that calling in sick a third of a year could be construed as more than just complacent but now wasn't the time to talk semantics.

DIM: Trev mate, you've been here fourteen years. You've survived how many restructures?

TREVOR: Five.

DIM: You're the cockroach that won't die no matter how many atom bombs they drop. Long live the cockroach!

TREVOR: Get out of here, Dim. Get out before it's too late and you're fifty with nothing to show for it except a stamp with your name misspelled.

CHORUS: Dim thought there was no way that could happen to him.

TREVOR: You're thinking there's no way that could happen to you.

CHORUS: Dim worried that he was too transparent.

TREVOR: I see right through you. You think you're twenty-seven—

DIM: Twenty-five.

TREVOR: You think you're twenty-seven and you've got all the time in the world to find what you really want. You don't. You're like all the other elephants who came here to die—slowly, one day at a time. And you won't be able to leave. There's long service—that dangling carrot—and you'll have a mortgage or a kid's orthodontic bills and the job market will be tight and you don't have experience doing anything else anyway and then you try to convince yourself, it's not so bad. It's not like you're sorting through sheep entrails. And that's what gets you to fifty with nothing to show for it except a youth spent formatting spreadsheets and listening to

TABITHA: That's right.

TREVOR: And

HEATHER: [*laughing*] Absolutely.

TREVOR: And you multiply that feeling by the number of people feeling it on every floor of every building in every city in the world and the sheer weight of human misery crushes you so you can't breathe and most of your waking time between masturbation and 'Black Books' is fantasising about filling your car with carbon dioxide only you don't have a car and your oven's electric so you have to throw yourself off a roof and be buried in a vacuum bag.

Beat.

I'm going to the loo.

DIM *stares at his computer, deeply disturbed.*

GRANT: You alright, mate?

DIM: What?

GRANT: You look like your cock just fell off. You okay?

DIM: Yeah.

CHORUS: Dim knows he has a couple of lines of fairly nasty speed in his pocket from the last time he wore these pants.

DIM: Just thinking about my future.

GRANT: Cheer up. There's good news.

CHORUS: Or should he nip across the road for a couple of Jägermeister shots?

GRANT: One day you'll be dead and you won't have to put up with this shit anymore.

DIM *stares at* GRANT.

CHORUS: Decision made.

He'll do the speed and the shots.

SCENE SEVEN

Outside the office. Under the stairwell.

NINA *and* TABITHA *are smoking.*

CHORUS: THE SMOKO.

The most-treasured ten minutes of the public sector workday.

Heather is so committed to observing the sanctity of the tea-break that she once put a post-it on her forehead that read, 'I'm on a break'

So no-one would disturb her with work-related matter.

NINA: You a good worker—we love you.

TABITHA: You'll love someone else.

NINA: Of course—but we love you now. Why?

TABITHA: Mum's getting worse. I'm looking at nursing homes but they want the house. My mother's house. I could rent somewhere I know but I've done all this reno work… And if we sold now we'd lose. Once the bank gets their mortgage back plus their seventeen pounds of flesh—I'd have to take out another bloody loan. If they'd give me one. It just happened so fast. She was Mum and suddenly she's not anymore. And I don't know, nursing homes—most places you wouldn't keep a cat—unless you really didn't like the cat. And I don't know that she's ready, you know—she still knows where she is. She gets to the toilet. The gas is off so she can't blow herself up. I don't want to do it while she still knows enough to hate me for it. And I saw this job going in Primary Industries and—

NINA: You applied?

TABITHA: Not yet.

NINA: With Sammy—you know— [*making the sign of the cross*] I'm new Deputy Manager, you be new me. Promotion, more responsibility—what more do you want?

CHORUS: Tabitha wanted somewhere quiet, dark and warm.

Under the covers of a bed in a country house away from mothers

Lovers

And Ukrainians.

NINA: You need the extra money. Everything is going to be better once I'm Deputy Manager—I promise.

TABITHA: I need something to change.

NINA: Change? Nothing change. Everywhere you go the same. Work. Home. There's always someone to bust your balls. At least at work there's no idiot to complain about his back and haemorrhoids.

CHORUS: Tabitha secretly enjoyed hearing about people's unhappy marriages.

There was a lady across the street from her house who often spoke of how she planned to suffocate her husband in his sleep.

TABITHA: So the sciatica still causing him trouble?

NINA: His brain is fucked up—that's problem. He can't keep his hands off me. All the time with the sex. Last night he want me to suck his cock.

TABITHA: Oh…

NINA: I asked when the last time you had a shower, Rene? You think I put that filthy slug in my mouth?

The sound of a text message.

TABITHA *checks her phone.*

I'm not twenty-three no more. No way, Jose.

CHORUS: Text message.

GRANT: Miaow. Can I stroke my little kitten in the archive compactus? I promise you a saucer of milk. X.X.

TABITHA: I need different faces—

NINA: Which face you don't like? Trevor? He's gone.

TABITHA: I need different work—

NINA: All work the same! Computer, Problem, Solve, Done, Next, Telephone, Problem, Solve, Next. We all get bored. We all get depressed.

TABITHA: You're depressed?

NINA: Of course! What can I do? Zoloft? Get fat? No.

TABITHA: I don't know how I can do another thirty years of this.

NINA: You don't think about it.

TABITHA: I fell asleep at my desk the other day. I don't know how long for.

CHORUS: She'd been asleep for twenty-seven minutes.

Dim stuck a post-it on her forehead that read, 'Honk if you're horny'.

NINA: I talk to upstairs. We move you up a level. More money.

TABITHA: It's not about money! It's about my mother who thought I was my dead sister this morning and wouldn't stop crying because I was 'alive'. It's termites in the stumps of a house I will never own but can't sell. It's hiding Johnny Walker under the bed, it's nothing good on television—it's everything! It's me! I want to unzip myself out of these thirty-three years and let someone else take over the carcass.

CHORUS: Tabitha didn't say any of that.

She'd been brought up to mostly say nothing.

Instead she said

TABITHA: Okay. I'll think about it.

SCENE EIGHT

A restaurant.

HEATHER *and* RICHARD *sit at a table.*

RICHARD: Pancreatic cancer?

HEATHER: Like Pavarotti.

RICHARD: You don't come back from pancreatic. It was breast cancer with Annie.

HEATHER: That's awful.

RICHARD: She had the left mastectomy and we thought we were safe. It's not that you can't have breast cancer without breasts. We just… she'd suffered enough. Thought we'd made a bargain with God. Take the boobs and leave her be.

He tries to chuckle as though this was a joke.

HEATHER: I'm so sorry, Richard.

RICHARD: She died and I thought… the world stopped. Couldn't make sense of anything. All these friends, neighbours, kept coming around with food. And I knew they meant well and were… concerned but… you're with someone nearly forty years you don't want a bloody plate of lasagne.

Beat.

Got so I didn't want to leave the house. Couldn't. I just didn't see the point of anything. It's like I'd died too only there'd been a mistake and somehow I was still around.

Beat.

God forgive me for saying it—but I decided to kill myself.

HEATHER: Oh, Richard.

RICHARD: I wrote letters to Katie and Rebecca and I went out to the garage. Took a coil of rope. Made the noose. Tied it to the ceiling beam. Stood on the chair and… it broke.

HEATHER: The rope?

RICHARD: The chair. The bloody leg just snapped. Put my back out.

HEATHER: I don't believe it!

RICHARD: Had to wait the entire night on that concrete floor until Ella—she's my neighbour—stuck her beak in the next morning.

HEATHER *laughs.*

HEATHER: I shouldn't laugh!

RICHARD: Why not? It's funny.

He refills her glass.

Have more wine.

HEATHER: You're getting me drunk.

RICHARD: We're adults.

HEATHER: Yes and I'd like to behave like one. I don't want to leave here with my skirt over my head.

RICHARD: Or urine down my trousers.

HEATHER *laughs.*

HEATHER: Stop it!

RICHARD: Hell, we're old. We'll just pretend we're senile.

HEATHER: The sad truth is they'd believe it.

They look at each other.

RICHARD: That chair breaking was a gift. I believe that. That was Annie telling me she was alright and I wasn't to do anything so stupid ever again. And I've been okay since.

HEATHER: I'm happy that chair broke.

RICHARD: Me too. A toast.

They raise their glasses.

HEATHER: To faulty furniture.

RICHARD: To shoddy carpenters everywhere.

They drink.

Your turn.

HEATHER: Lordy.

RICHARD: It's not that bad, is it?

HEATHER: Just boring.

RICHARD: I don't believe you. Heather MacIntosh—sorry, Miller—was never boring.

HEATHER: That may have been the case forty years ago but times have definitely changed.

RICHARD: You remember that party at Torquay?

HEATHER: Which one?

RICHARD: You know which one.

HEATHER *blushes.*

HEATHER: Richard, please. I'm a grandmother, for Christ sakes.

RICHARD: I heard about your marriage.

HEATHER: Oh.

RICHARD: I'm sorry.

HEATHER: These things happen all the time.

RICHARD: Still… It must've been distressing for you.

HEATHER: It was a bit of an adjustment at first.

RICHARD: I completely understand.

Pause.

Was it an amicable separation?

HEATHER: It was a divorce and—no.

RICHARD: I'm sorry, I'm prying.

HEATHER: Not at all. He left me. For a younger woman. After twenty-three years and five children. Even saying it is embarrassing. 'A younger woman'. The worst cliché.

Pause.

RICHARD: Was it a good marriage?

HEATHER: Apparently not.

RICHARD: I'm sorry. That was a stupid thing to say—I'm sorry.

HEATHER: I wasn't expecting it. You think you're supposed to know, there are meant to be signs. And then your husband tells you he's leaving you for his receptionist and it's like… someone's dropped a piano on your head. That's what's so embarrassing. Being one of *those* women.

RICHARD: Those women?

HEATHER: The ones who don't know their husband is screwing the ugly receptionist. That I can't forgive him for. Younger is one thing. But ugly? I've seen turds with more charisma.

Beat.

Sorry.

RICHARD: Don't apologise

HEATHER: Screw him. And his nasty turd wife. Wanting my grandchild to be his flower girl—the balls!

Beat.

Sorry.

RICHARD: He's an idiot. I can't imagine ever wanting to leave you.

HEATHER *is uncomfortable.*

HEATHER: Well…

RICHARD: That party at Torquay. You were chasing Arthur Hewitt.

HEATHER: Who?

RICHARD: Arthur Hewitt. Tall boy. Red hair?

HEATHER: I have no idea who you're talking about. I was chasing him?

RICHARD: You told me you were in love with him.

HEATHER: Really? Red hair?

RICHARD: We were sitting on the swings and you told me you were in love with him.

HEATHER: Lordy. I can't remember him at all. Was he one of Mitch's friends?

RICHARD: Broke my heart.

HEATHER: What are you talking about?

RICHARD: Heather, didn't you know I was in love with you?

Beat.

HEATHER: You're joking.

RICHARD: I was mad about you.

HEATHER: Don't come the prawn!

RICHARD: When you told me about Arthur… I couldn't say anything then. I left the next day—didn't you wonder why I'd left?

HEATHER: Are you really telling the truth?

RICHARD: The next time we saw each other—must've been more than ten years—we were both married then.

HEATHER: Why didn't you say anything?

RICHARD: You were in love with Arthur.

HEATHER: Arthur? Oh God, Richard—some git I don't even remember. Why tell me now? When I'm too old and fat to do anything about it?

RICHARD: Why can't we do something about it?

Beat.

HEATHER: What are you talking about?

RICHARD: We're both single.

HEATHER: Single? Oh, Richard, don't be stupid.

RICHARD: Why's it stupid?

HEATHER: I'm fifty-seven, Richard.

RICHARD: And I'm sixty-one—so?

HEATHER: Jesus!

RICHARD: What's the matter? Why are you getting so upset?

HEATHER: This isn't *The Golden Girls*, Richard! I don't go around… dating!

RICHARD: Where's the harm in two friends seeing each other?

CHORUS: If Heather could have articulated why she was feeling this overwhelming sense of panic, she would have said

HEATHER: No-one has shown any interest in me—romantically speaking—in about… God, I can't even remember. But it was a different decade. I'm so fat and ugly. My bum's an old peach, my boobs half-filled sacks of grain, the caesarean scars—Jesus, all of it disgusts me. I haven't masturbated in two years because I find it so… depressing. I'm sorry, Richard. But the thought of anyone seeing me naked, let alone… touching me… I think I'm going to be sick.

CHORUS: Instead Heather said

HEATHER *stands.*

HEATHER: I think it's time to go home.

RICHARD: But… we've got pudding!

HEATHER: Cancel it. I'm not hungry.

RICHARD: Heather, I'm sorry. I didn't mean to offend you, I'm sorry. Please—

HEATHER: You haven't offended me, Richard. Don't act the banana.

RICHARD: But—

HEATHER: I'm tired and we've had too much wine. I just want to go home.

Pause.

RICHARD: Okay.

CHORUS: They didn't speak on the drive home.

Not about anything important.

RICHARD: Of course it's the Asians you can't compete with. Bloody Chinese, Indonesia, Taiwan.

HEATHER: Grace is six but still not talking much.

RICHARD: They just produce everything so much cheaper and they got an endless labour force working for peanuts.

HEATHER: If you ask me she's a bit slow but I can't tell my daughter anything.

CHORUS: Richard walked Heather to the door.

She gave him a peck on the cheek and said

HEATHER: Goodnight.

RICHARD: Goodnight.

CHORUS: Richard drove a little way down the street—just far enough so Heather couldn't see him from her window.

He turned off the engine

And stared at the steering wheel

Feeling lonelier and older than he had felt in a long time.

SCENE NINE

The office.

HEATHER, GRANT, TREVOR, TABITHA *and* NINA *stand together, each reading the same document.*

DIM *sits at his desk. He is on the phone.*

CHORUS: THE PROBLEM WITH CHANGE.

No-one has anything against change

Not per se

No

It's just these management types cook up *finger quote* 'good ideas' *end finger quote* like

GRANT: Alcohol-free zones? Not again.

CHORUS: In their ivory tower with their mini-muffins and filtered coffee, but it's the troops on the frontline who suffer with

NINA: Police and local business liaison

HEATHER: Liquor licensing revisions

TABITHA: Community mail-out

TREVOR: On-street signage

GRANT: Warning surrounding councils that our drunks are moving in.

DIM: [*on the phone*] Tran? Tran, will ya just listen? Fuck girlfriends! Pissed chicks at pubs love drummers! Your hands will be so wet with poontang you'll reek of fish for weeks! Man—

HEATHER: They won't really fine the boongs for drinking in Kellaway Park, will they?

TABITHA: You're really not supposed to call them that, Heather.

HEATHER: After all the work we've done making them blacks part of our community—

NINA: The plaque.

CHORUS: Nina is referring to the Kellaway Park plaque, which commemorates the contribution past and present made by the community's Indigenous people.

HEATHER: And now they can't even get sloshed around it.

GRANT: They'll think we're racist.

TABITHA: We are racist.

GRANT: Yes, but now they'll *know* we are. That's management for you. Lack of big picture thinking.

TABITHA: Don't you mean, lack of little picture thinking? Because they don't think through the details?

GRANT: It's a lack of big picture, little picture—it's a complete lack of picture.

Beat.

And thinking.

DIM: [*on the phone*] Yeah, I know, I know Mules leaving left a bit of a hole— [*Beat.*] Alright, a fucking crater then! But he's not the only talent in this band.

TREVOR: We don't have time for this.

HEATHER: I'm staying back nights as it is.

CHORUS: Heather, along with everyone else, stays at work until 5:23 p.m.—the minimum daily overtime necessary to accrue a monthly RDO.

She spends those twenty-three minutes plucking her eyebrows using her monitor as a mirror.

DIM: [*on the phone*] I believe in this new direction for Roy 23. Enough with that soft melancholic 'I'm-fucking-alone-in-a-disconnected-fucked-up-planet-where's-the-meaning?' shit, man—we're not fucking Coldplay—the kids want a harder sound—with anger and balls, man. We're on the cusp of a grunge revival!

TREVOR: Look at my calendar! Chockas!

CHORUS: Trevor's Outlook calendar does appear to be full of meetings. But if you clicked on any of those meetings you'd find something like this

Eleven o'clock—Mr Espresso.

Twelve o'clock—Mr Lunch.

One o'clock—Mr Grey (as in, the Earl).

Two to five o'clock—Busy.

Which means Trevor will alternate between the loo regretting his life choices and his desk looking at YouTube mash-ups of animals attacking humans.

DIM: [*on the phone*] We've been working on this band three years, man—you're gonna throw that away for what? For software fucking engineering? To be another fucking Asian working in IT? You're better than that, man. We're better than that.

NINA: We'll get calls. Complaints. Tabitha, make sure to update the IVR.

GRANT: Press '4' to find out where you have to endure your family's company without grog. Christ.

HEATHER: The phone won't stop ringing as it is.

Everyone stares at the phone.

Beat.

It rings.

HEATHER *answers it.*

DDD—Oh hello, love. [*Beat.*] Absolute bedlam as usual. You know how it is around here. [*Beat.*] No, I can talk.

DIM: [*on the phone*] You're not s'pose to give up until your thirties, man—your twenties is the last place you can dream, dude. You got the rest of your life to sell out and be depressed by the what could've beens.

GRANT: You know what'll happen, don't you? Just like last time, and the time before that. We'll break our backs getting it all done and then in a year they'll chuck it all out and make us change it back. Why do we bother?

CHORUS: No-one realised Grant did bother.

Everyone returns to their desk.

DIM: [*on the phone*] Tran—Tran—we need this band. Without it we're just… like all the other dudes who used to be in a band.

Beat.

DIM *puts the phone down.*

CHORUS: No-one has anything against change
Not per se
It's just nothing really does change
No-one has time for it
It's always worse
And the way things are is always better.

TABITHA: That's right.

HEATHER: [*laughing*] Absolutely.

SCENE TEN

Sammy's house. The production line.

HEATHER *cuts cake.* TABITHA *holds a glass of water in which* HEATHER *dips the knife after cutting each slice.* NINA *holds plates, upon which* HEATHER *plops cake.*

NINA *passes the cake to* TREVOR.

TREVOR *spoons on double cream and passes the cake to* DIM.

DIM *places a fork on the plate and passes to* GRANT.

GRANT *passes the cake to* LACHLAN. LACHLAN *passes the cake back to* HEATHER *and so on until every team member has a piece of cake with cream and fork.*

CHORUS: THE LONG GOODBYE.
HR Policy Document 17.6—'Dealing with a terminally ill employee'.
Bullet point: Keep relationships as normal as possible.
People become very awkward when they talk to the sick person.
They're afraid the fatally ill person will break down and cry.
The natural sense of camaraderie that once existed disappears.
The afflicted employee ends up feeling rebuffed.
Don't ignore the fatally ill employee.
Arrange a card

Arrange flowers
Arrange a visit.

HEATHER: I love these curtains.

TABITHA: They're nice, aren't they?

TREVOR: They are nice.

CHORUS: Remember—they're still a member of the team
And they matter.
Be supportive.
Be compassionate.
Try to keep the conversation light.

DIM: Hey, I'll give you twenty bucks for one of those Percocet.

Everyone laughs.

LACHLAN: So how you feeling, Sammy?

GRANT: You look good.

CHORUS: He looks awful.

GRANT: Maybe not good enough to run a marathon.

LACHLAN: But you look good.

HEATHER: Where did you get them from? The curtains?

NINA: Shut up about the fucking curtains.

HEATHER: I'm just making conversation.

LACHLAN: So how do you feel?

GRANT: [*whispering*] Stop staring.

DIM: [*whispering*] Was I staring?

CHORUS: Try not to notice the smell
The smell the dying get
Cancer breath when their insides start rotting.

DIM: [*whispering*] He's a bit yellow isn't he?

TREVOR: [*whispering*] Didn't think he'd look so bad.

LACHLAN: You look good. You look really good.

CHORUS: A month ago he looked like… Sammy.

Now he looks…

Silence.

NINA: Work's… work.

TABITHA: It always is, isn't it?

HEATHER: We've had a bit of a backlash—

DIM: A fucking torrential flood more like—

GRANT: A tsunami of hate—

HEATHER: Against the new parking restrictions on Kelly Street.

TABITHA: Someone mailed in a turd.

NINA: Fucking bastards.

TABITHA: A bloody turd.

GRANT: Poor Heather opened it.

HEATHER: Thank goodness I'm not precious.

LACHLAN: We can't just let people park anywhere.

TABITHA: Do as they please.

NINA: Double-park.

TREVOR: Triple-park.

HEATHER: For as long as they like.

GRANT: To hell with the residents.

LACHLAN: It'd be chaos.

NINA: This isn't Italy.

CHORUS: Try not to notice that smell.

TABITHA: Can someone open a window or something?

DIM: Or get a Glade thingy-mi-jig?

CHORUS: Try not to notice the colostomy bag.

DIM: [*whispering*] Jesus, can't he even use the toilet anymore?

NINA: Shh!

HEATHER: Let me help you with that.

GRANT: [*whispering*] Stop staring.

HEATHER: This is a good pillow. So firm. What's that made out of?

DIM: [*whispering*] Was I staring?

HEATHER: Moulded foam? I need new pillows.

NINA: Stop trying to steal his pillows.

HEATHER: I'm just making conversation.

DIM: How're the drugs? Any good?

TABITHA: Oh, Christ!

HEATHER: Don't be embarrassed—it's just a little sick sick.

DIM: That's morphine for ya.

HEATHER: Goodness, with five kids the number of times I've been thrown up on. You lose count, don't you?

GRANT: The Pies are doing well, aren't they? See them against Geelong?

CHORUS: A month ago he was still… Sammy.

And now he's…

TABITHA: So happy we came.

HEATHER: Of course we came. We had to come.

CHORUS: Try not to notice how much he wants you to piss off.

Try not to think of how he's got—what, another week? Maybe two?

And he has to spend it with dickheads being jolly.

Making conversation about the curtains.

And the pillows.

TREVOR: Yeah, we're having a really good time.

Beat.

I didn't mean for that to come out sarcastic—if it came out sarcastic—I didn't mean that. Really. This is fun.

Silence.

LACHLAN: Tell us how you made this cake, Heather.

HEATHER: Bought it from the shop. Sorry, Sammy—I was going to make my tiramisu that you like but I ran out of time and… it's all calories, isn't it?

LACHLAN: Well… it's delicious.

CHORUS: It's not.

LACHLAN takes a big bite.

LACHLAN: Yum yum.

TABITHA cries.

Everyone is trying not to cry.

NINA: [*whispering*] If you don't stop crying I'll stab you with this fork. Stop it!

TABITHA: Hay fever.

HEATHER: Have a Claratyne, love.

CHORUS: Try not to notice how his tongue hangs out of his mouth like a tiny curtain of dead meat
Try not to notice his faraway eyes looking through you
Try not to notice he's dying.

Ella Caldwell (left) as Tabitha and Andrea Swifte as Heather in the 2010 production at Red Stitch Actors Theatre in Melbourne. (Photo: Jodie Hutchinson)

SCENE ELEVEN

The office.

CHORUS: THE TEAM MEETING.

An exercise in excruciating tedium.

Agenda

Minutes

Heather accusing Trevor of stealing her Penang curry

Trevor almost in tears denying it

While Dim

The actual curry thief

Fantasises about being a secret agent who is deep

Way deep

Undercover as a bored administrator when the henchmen of his nemesis barge into the meeting and expose his true identity forcing him to abseil down the building and flee.

But this meeting is different…

HEATHER: Oh, my turn. Well… let's see. Okay, I've got a good one. Lordy. The first time I met Sammy was when he interviewed me—this was when I first started at DDDPTS in registration—and I was wearing my checked suit and he said, 'I hope it's just your suit and not your past that's checkered'.

Polite laughter.

Yes—you could count on Sammy to say something funny.

CHORUS: This wasn't true.

Most people considered Sammy humourless and he was such a chronic low-talker that if he did crack a joke—no-one heard it.

NINA: Grant?

GRANT: I don't know I have a specific Sammy moment. None that he would have particularly liked me to share.

CHORUS: Grant once found norgs-as-big-as-jugs.com in Sammy's internet cache.

GRANT: But I enjoyed talking footy with him on a Monday morning. He was misguided of course as all Collingwood fans are—

Polite laughter.

But I knew him a long time. There's not many people I can say have been here longer than me but Sammy's one of them. He worked hard. At least in the early years before he became management—

CHORUS: One of the core tenets of the workplace is that management is always

Stupid

Incompetent

EVERYONE: And wouldn't know a hard day's work if it bit them in the bum!

Polite laughter.

GRANT: He paid off his mortgage. He was proud of that. And he loved his footy.

CHORUS: Something else Sammy loved (though the team never knew it) was Soviet history

He planned on visiting Moscow when he retired

And he would stand in the Red Square

Remembering the great military parades he had seen as a boy in black-and-white when the world was divided in two

He imagined standing before Saint Basil's Cathedral, its onion domes in golds, pinks and blues

The inspiration for the faraway kingdom of princesses, witches and dragons in the sagas he wrote when he was eleven.

NINA: He was a good Father Christmas. Very funny. With the ho-hos. Remember?

HEATHER: He was a great Father Christmas!

GRANT: He had the build for it, didn't he?

TREVOR: Loved his food.

Polite laughter.

DIM: Not in the end he didn't.

The laughter stops.

CHORUS: In his last week

When he was fed protein and salt intravenously whilst drifting in and out of consciousness

Sammy longed for his mother's Bacalhau à Gomes de Sá

Salt cod with potatoes, eggs and olives

It wasn't food he wanted but the taste of the familiar

The taste that went with being slapped for nicking a hardboiled egg

Running hot and dirty through summer streets

Spitting orange pips at his brothers.

TABITHA: Remember that time he got drunk at the Christmas party on the boat and he vomited off the side thinking none of us could see and then he denied it? And he had little specks of vomit on his tie! He was so embarrassed!

Polite laughter.

HEATHER: Wasn't that Kirk? From Systems?

NINA: It was Kirk I think. The little one. Filipino?

TABITHA: Really?

GRANT: I thought it was the other Kirk—the fat one—from Financial Ops?

TABITHA: I heard it was Sammy. I don't know. I wasn't even there.

Beat.

NINA: Trevor? You have a story to share about Sammy?

TREVOR: I worked with him for fourteen years. And I never asked about his accent.

GRANT: He was Spanish.

NINA: No, Portuguese.

GRANT: Oh.

NINA: But he didn't like Nandos. I never understood.

CHORUS: Samuél de Menezes emigrated to Australia in 1979 when he was twenty years old

He spoke four languages fluently

Portuguese, English, Spanish and French

A week before his diagnosis he had ordered Rosetta Stone to learn Russian.

He never opened the box.

TREVOR: I should've made an effort to know him better. He was a good egg. A very good, very decent egg.

CHORUS: Sammy had once found Trevor crying in a toilet cubicle.

Trevor had accidentally invoiced one thousand and eight-three people erroneously and was convinced he would be sacked for gross negligence.

Sammy cancelled the invoices from the system and never said a word about it to anyone.

And after having made Trevor explain exactly what had happened

Sammy never mentioned it to him again either.

TREVOR: I want you to know that you're all good eggs. The best eggs. And I'm lucky to know all of you. This entire experience—seeing what happened to Sammy… I'm going to change. Everything. I've wasted the first fifty years of my life—

DIM: Forty-eight.

TREVOR: And I'm not going to waste any more.

Beat.

I'm in love with a parking inspector who's also named Trevor!

Beat.

HEATHER: [*to* TREVOR] Have a scone, love.

NINA: Dim, you've only been here a year—

DIM: Fourteen months.

NINA: That long? Where does the time go?

DIM *stares blankly at* NINA.

What do you want to say about Sammy?

CHORUS: Dim wanted to say…

DIM: I didn't know him that well. None of us did. He was kinda quiet. Shy. If he saw you in the kitchen he'd come back later to make his tea because he hated small talk. I liked that about him. He didn't do small talk. I don't know how he did it. Coming in here for thirty years. Did anyone think that it was the thirty years before the cancer that was the real tragedy? Moving shit from in-tray to out-tray until the pile gets so big you can't be bothered filing so you chuck it all in the confidential recycling bin. Summarising tables of tables, summarising reports on the impact of metered parking that no-one will ever read. The meetings on the same issues that have been discussed for the last seven meetings. Everyone actually believing that they are busier than everyone else. The emails that cc you when you don't need to be cc'd. Most days I do nothing except think of rude puns on how to sign off emails I send my fuck bunny like Captain Huge and Boy Cumder. And when I think about this being the rest of my life… I need more than just… activity. I need to be more than just another hamster running the same stupid wheel. I want to actually achieve something. Something small… but something! Anything!

Beat.

Everyone is stunned by DIM*'s outburst.*

Everyone looks to CHORUS.

CHORUS: That's what Dim wanted to say…

And that's exactly what he did say.

DIM: [*looking at* CHORUS] Shit.

DIM *looks at the team who stare at him appalled.*

He starts to leave the room but returns to collect a packet of Cheds crackers.

He runs out.

TREVOR: If he resigns I'm bagsing his desk.

SCENE TWELVE

Outside the office. Under the stairwell.

DIM *is binging on Cheds crackers.*

GRANT *approaches.*

DIM: Before you get all sooky la-la on me I know I got carried—

GRANT: Turn around.

DIM: What?

GRANT: Turn around.

Beat.

DIM: No, you weirdo—

GRANT *forcibly tries to turn* DIM *around to kick him in the bum.*

Get off me, / you fucking maniac! Stop touching my arse!

GRANT: You little turd! Stop it! Stand still, you shit!

DIM *manages to break away.*

DIM: Have you lost your fucking mind?

GRANT: You're finished for today. You come in tomorrow and you apologise to those people. You're young and stupid. Overcome with grief. You said things you didn't mean. Some shit like that. But you make it sincere and you say it nice. And I want you in a suit. Looking professional. You understand?

DIM: I was gonna apologise before you got all homoerotic, you fucking… dick!

GRANT: Do you think you're the only one who's ever felt that way? Feeling shit about their job, their life. 'What else is there?' You miserable little snot! Everyone feels like that! And we get the fuck on with it! Everyone in there gets the fuck on with it and we do it with as much dignity as we can!

CHORUS: Well… no-one had ever accused Trevor of dignity but now was not the time to qualify grand statements.

TABITHA *enters.*

GRANT *and* DIM *do not see her.*

She listens.

GRANT: And I don't need some pimply little teenager like you talking out your bumhole down on me.

DIM: I didn't mean it like—

GRANT: What the fuck do you know about happiness? When you've got kids and Foxtel and calisthenics and everything costs money and what you want doesn't matter. What it takes to keep… doing it. What the fuck do you know about anything?

DIM: I was just saying a man spent thirty years of his life doing… and he ends up a yellow skeleton crumpled over with back pain and diarrhoea. It's… y'know, tragic.

GRANT: How do you think you're gonna end up? No-one gets out of here a happy old man asleep on a pair of 20-year-old tits. The exit looks a lot more like a colostomy bag, sick down your front, surrounded by arseholes making stupid jokes about Percocet.

DIM: I was tryna lighten the mood! Thought the poor bastard could do with a laugh—

GRANT: You were tryna score his drugs, you shit!

DIM: He doesn't need them now, does he?

Beat.

C'mon, big fella, I'm sorry, alright? I'm a cunt and you're an arsehole, okay—friends?

GRANT: You can't just sum up a life like that. Make it sound like it didn't count for anything.

DIM: I didn't—

GRANT: It's a man's life, you fucking snot! A man—not a bloody hamster.

GRANT *stares* DIM *down.*

GRANT *leaves.*

DIM *calls after him.*

DIM: Big fella… I'm sorry!

Beat.

TABITHA *approaches.*

She lights a cigarette.

TABITHA: You alright?

DIM: Does everyone hate me?

TABITHA: You know this place. Everyone loves a bit of controversy—breaks up the day. There was a guy about three years ago—Martin. He was on the phone and he just went ballistic. Screaming, 'You fucking wog maggot! I know where you live! I know where you live!' And then he took off his pants and tried to go to sleep under his desk. They needed security to get him out. It was all anyone could talk about for weeks.

Beat.

Heather thinks you're in shock because of Sammy and Trevor thinks you need counselling and has a number you can call and Nina doesn't care as long as you do your job and Grant thinks… No-one hates you.

DIM: What do you think?

TABITHA: I think… I think that's the best meeting I've ever been to.

DIM: Really?

TABITHA: I would love to have done that. Just scream. Everything. Scream and scream until there's nothing left. And you just did it.

DIM: What would you scream?

TABITHA: Oh…

CHORUS: If she were being honest, Tabitha would scream something like

TABITHA: How the law of inertia explains my whole life. How I've always been this stationary object waiting for a net external force that's never coming and I'm drowning, I'm drowning, I'm fucking drowning and haven't got the first idea how to stop drowning.

CHORUS: But Tabitha is not being honest, so she says

TABITHA: I'd scream… something stupid about the photocopier never working or finishing a report about a project that management scrapped a year ago but no-one told me. The usual things.

DIM: I didn't mean to call you a hamster.

TABITHA: I am a hamster. I just don't mind as much as you do.

DIM: Why not?

TABITHA: It's not building mud huts in Guatemala but it matters, you know. Footpath trading matters to people. DAMP—

CHORUS: The Domestic Animal Management Plan—

TABITHA: —matters. You're not going to put it on your gravestone but it matters. Someone has to do it.

DIM: Do you think they'll sack me?

TABITHA: It's the DDDPTS, Dim. You could set the building on fire and they wouldn't sack you.

DIM: What about Martin? The guy with no pants?

TABITHA: He resigned. I heard he's doing holistic medicine in Warrandyte. Do you want to be sacked?

DIM: This is only temporary, you know. Music is still my main thing.

TABITHA: Of course.

DIM: But the pay's good.

TABITHA: Yeah.

DIM: Conditions are good.

TABITHA: I know.

DIM: People are good.

TABITHA: Absolutely.

DIM: There are worse jobs. A mate of mine works for an accounting firm and they found out he could play guitar so now he has to go in on Sunday mornings to play the *Mamma Mia* soundtrack with the company band.

TABITHA: That's horrific.

DIM: What did you wanna do? When you were little?

TABITHA: It's just a job, Dim. It's not you.

DIM: You're not gonna tell me?

TABITHA: I never really thought about it. I wanted a husband and children and a house and a job where I got to wear high heels and tight skirts and type letters on typewriters—not computers. That beautiful tat-tat-tat sound you only get with a typewriter. And when I was older I wanted more or less the same things, but you know—more politically correct. I'd work in an office but I wouldn't be the secretary and I'd have a husband but he would sometimes cook. Less 1950s—more 1990s. But it was really the same thing. Just different hairstyles.

DIM: And now?

TABITHA: What about now?

DIM: Is this what you want?

TABITHA: It's fine. I'm fine.

DIM: No you're not.

TABITHA: Excuse me?

DIM: I don't believe you.

DIM *and* TABITHA *stare at each other.*

Beat.

TABITHA: I just came to see that you were okay.

DIM: Don't go.

TABITHA: This isn't going to happen.

DIM: Why not?

TABITHA: You're a baby.

DIM: I'm twenty-five.

TABITHA: I'm too old for you.

DIM: You're thirty? Thirty-one?

TABITHA: I'm thirty-three and I'm not doing this.

DIM: Yes you are.

DIM *kisses* TABITHA.

TABITHA: This is not going to happen.

DIM: It's too late. It's already happening.

Beat.

TABITHA *kisses* DIM *back.*

She pulls away.

TABITHA: But why?

DIM: What?

TABITHA: Me. Why do you want this with me?

DIM: Because… I don't feel like… such a loser. With you.

TABITHA: Is that because you consider me a bigger loser?

DIM: Not fully.

TABITHA *pulls away.*

No wait, that came out stupid. I mean… you don't make me feel like a failure. You don't make me feel like I'm supposed to be something better than this. It's like… you're a civilian and you think it's okay, like I'm okay… being a civilian.

TABITHA: I think you mean that to be sweet.

CHORUS: What Tabitha means is

TABITHA: I'm already in a sexual relationship with a man whose self-esteem I'm bolstering and I'm fucking exhausted.

CHORUS: But what Tabitha says is

TABITHA: Look, Dim, we'd have rushed and… quite likely awkward sex two, three times—

CHORUS: Dim was hoping

At best

For a little reciprocated genital fondling in the car park—he had no idea sex on multiple occasions was on the table.

TABITHA: And then we would be awkward and embarrassed and ashamed… until you, or I, find someone else to do that with and then we'd pretend it never happened and what's the point really?

DIM: I've already got someone to do that with.

TABITHA: Oh.

DIM: I'm not looking for another fuck bunny.

TABITHA: Oh.

Beat.

Me neither.

Beat.

DIM: So…?

TABITHA: So?

DIM: We'll just like each other then.

TABITHA: Okay.

DIM: We don't need to sleep with each other because we have no-one else to sleep with.

TABITHA: No.

DIM: We can like each other.

TABITHA: Yes.

Beat.

We can like each other.

They smile.

SCENE THIRTEEN

The office.

NINA *is in a meeting with* LACHLAN.

LACHLAN: I'd like to thank you for the way you've stepped up over the last little while when we really needed you to.

NINA: No problem.

LACHLAN: I know we've had our differences in the past—

CHORUS: Nina once stormed out of a meeting after calling Lachlan a fucking idiot.

NINA: I say what I think.

LACHLAN: I know you do.

CHORUS: Lachlan thinks Nina is Eastern bloc trash but he'd still like to fuck her

From behind

Over a desk

With her undies around her ankles.

LACHLAN: But I want you to know that I really value your contribution to this organisation. You're one of those people who can be relied on to get the job done.

NINA: Thank you.

CHORUS: Nina still thinks Lachlan is a fucking idiot.

LACHLAN: You've got a tremendous work ethic. No-one else in the public service turns up to work when they've got pneumonia.

NINA: They don't do anything when they turn up anyway.

Polite laughter.

LACHLAN: As you know, Nina—with Sam's unexpected passing—that the position of Deputy Manager is now vacant. You've been acting in that position—and very well too, I might say. Sammy used to joke that you were this department and everyone else was just decoration.

NINA: Sammy was so funny. But that's true.

LACHLAN: You know the system, the processes inside out. You're analytical, you're bright—you're cleverer than most people in any given situation. Nina, I know this probably comes as a surprise but… we will not be offering you the position of Deputy Manager.

CHORUS: Nina thinks she has turnips instead of ears.

NINA: What?

LACHLAN: You're just not… management material.

CHORUS: It'll happen to them like it did with the Agbaje family in their block of flats. Quietly. No-one will even notice until they see Unit 14 for sale.

And then it will be the beginning. Starting with nothing.

Again.

LACHLAN: Your manner is… so direct. In fact you can be quite rude. I've had several complaints about your tone and choice of language.

NINA: Trevor?

LACHLAN: I have to maintain the confidence of employees who've stepped forward.

CHORUS: Which meant Trevor.

LACHLAN: Being a manager is about more than just knowing everything. In fact you don't really need to know anything as a manager. As long as you can manage. It's about people skills. It's about attending meetings with other heads of department and being able to communicate your point of view without… resorting to name-calling.

CHORUS: The only name Nina is calling over and over again in her head right now is her own.

Ninotchka, Ninotchka…

LACHLAN: And we all respect the way you've come to this country and really applied yourself. I know you started out in this department working for free—filing—just so you could have the opportunity to learn English and now you're a team leader. That's very impressive. I really do take my hat off to you. You're a very impressive woman, Nina.

CHORUS: Ninotchka, Ninotchka…

LACHLAN: But your grammar, your spelling… Being a manager means signing off on memos, writing policy reports, correspondence, presentations. You just don't have those skills—not at this level.

CHORUS: Ninotchka…

LACHLAN: We're offering the position of Deputy Manager to Tabitha. It's a big step up but she's been here eight years, she's competent, she's diligent, and she's due… some encouragement. I know it may be difficult to work under someone you used to manage. But she's going to need you at her side. She's going to need your support, your guidance, your knowledge. Sam was right. You are this department and everyone else is just decoration. I know you're probably disappointed but it was a case of the best candidate for the role. Do you understand?

Beat.

NINA *gets up and walks away.*

Before she leaves she turns to LACHLAN.

NINA: You are a fucking idiot!

SCENE FOURTEEN

Tabitha's bedroom.

GRANT: I've left Rachel.

CHORUS: Blunt opening.

Cut to her close-up.

TABITHA: What?

GRANT: Just now. Told her everything and drove straight over.

Beat.

GRANT *is hugging a sock.*

TABITHA: What's that?

GRANT: It's a sock. It's ours. All of it.

GRANT *pulls crumpled money out of the sock.*

CHORUS: Sweetly eccentric or overtly pathetic?

TABITHA: Jesus.

GRANT: I love you.

Beat.

TABITHA: I don't think you're feeling well.

GRANT: I love you.

Beat.

TABITHA: Grant, please—

GRANT: I love you I love you I love you. I love you. I love you. You're the—this is… this is the crazy burning crazy passionate love that you think only exists in the movies. I feel it! This is what they write about in songs. I can't breathe without you. I want to spend the rest of my life with you. I want to take care of you. Not in an overbearing, you know, aggressive masculine way but however you want me to. I know I'm not what you dreamed of. I'm married. I've got two kids. I've only got this sock. But I will devote the rest of my life to making you happy. I love you.

CHORUS: Not as good as the speech he did in the car but…

Good, good.

Beat.

TABITHA: I don't think you've thought this through.

GRANT: That's just it! I haven't thought about anything else for months and I've finally bloody worked it out. Each of us is just hanging by a thread waiting for the chop and when I die it's gonna be with a big smile on my face and you in my arms and not in a living room full of shit I never wanted to pay for.

CHORUS: She's melting.

Hands fluttering.

Nervous tears.

Be tender.

TABITHA: You love Rachel—you do.

GRANT: I've never loved her. Not the way I love you.

TABITHA: Then why did you marry her?

GRANT: Because… you're with someone and after a certain time that's… what you do. Rachel isn't the victim here—she doesn't love me either. Ask her. I'm forty-three years old and I'm in love. For the first time. I didn't think it would happen, I didn't believe in it. I thought it was something, you know, this big bullshit con they use to sell overpriced dinners on Valentine's Day.

TABITHA: You have two kids together, years together. You can't rub out all that history, you can't run away from your life!

GRANT: People do all the time. You either run away from your life or it runs away from you.

CHORUS: That sounded good. That's the tagline on the poster.

'You either run away from your life or it runs away from you.'

What does that mean exactly?

It's a tagline—it doesn't have to mean anything.

TABITHA: Grant… you didn't say anything stupid, did you? To Rachel? Nothing you couldn't take back?

GRANT: I don't want to take it back. I've left. The drive over here, I had my heart in my throat, scared to death what you'd say but… I've never felt so elated, so hopeful in my whole life.

CHORUS: Dip her in a passionate embrace.

She laughs

She cries

She swoons

Dolly in for the dip!

Cut to black!

'The End' in cursive font!

Pause.

GRANT: Tabby? Tabby, what are you thinking? Tell me.

TABITHA: This wasn't supposed to happen.

GRANT: Life—it gets complicated.

CHORUS: Zing!

Even better tagline.

TABITHA: I don't love you.

Beat.

GRANT: You're scared, I'm scared—

TABITHA: That's not it.

GRANT: You don't trust this, you don't believe you deserve love—

TABITHA: No, I believe I do deserve it, sort of, but it still won't happen, but no, that's not it. I'm sorry but I don't… love you.

CHORUS: And that's the kick to the nads right there.

GRANT: Not even… not even a bit?

TABITHA: This was very simple for me, Grant—I knew what this was and I never thought it was anything else. I told you this wasn't a great love affair. It was… you know, feeling beautiful occasionally. Desired even. Less lonely.

Beat.

I never lied to you. I never meant to mislead you… I kept telling you!

Beat.

GRANT*'s head is down. He cannot look up.*

I'm sorry. Grant? Grant, are you okay?

Pause.

Grant?

CHORUS: If Grant's heart wasn't breaking and he could speak without crying

He'd probably say

CHORUS *looks at* GRANT *who still cannot look up.*

Pause.

Well… sometimes there's nothing you can say.

SCENE FIFTEEN

Heather's bedroom.

HEATHER *stares at herself in the mirror.*

She presses her face. She lifts her boobs.

She stares for a long time.

She picks up the phone, dials a number, never taking her eyes off her reflection.

HEATHER: [*on the phone*] Richard? Hello, it's Heather. Miller. Mackintosh. Heather Miller. Yes. [*She laughs.*] That's me. Thought I'd take the bull by the undies and give you a call. I was wondering… [*Beat.*] Could we, if you're not too busy and so inclined, could we… would you like to try dinner again? I think I may have been a bit of a silly cucumber. [*Beat.*] Oh. [*Beat.*] Oh, of course. No, don't apologise. [*Beat.*] I understand. [*Beat.*] If that's how you feel, of course. [*Beat.*] Goodbye.

She hangs up the phone.

Long pause.

She dials a number.

[*on the phone*] Hi, Richard, it's me again. [*Beat.*] Yes, I'm sorry to call but… I'm not taking no for an answer. I acted like an idiot and I understand your reservations but no, I'm not taking no for an answer. I think we should have dinner because we'll have a good time and then maybe we'll have dinner again and another good time and maybe those good times will add up to something I don't know but we're not going to find out sitting at home with hurt feelings so this Friday, Giorgio's? You know it? [*Beat.*] Seven p.m? [*Beat. She smiles.*] Well, that sounds lovely.

SCENE SIXTEEN

The office. The production line.

NINA *hands* TABITHA *plastic cups which she pours juice into.* TABITHA *passes the filled cups to* DIM, *who passes them onto* TREVOR, *who passes them onto* HEATHER, *who passes them onto* GRANT *until everyone has a half-filled cup of juice.*

CHORUS: THE FAREWELL.

A card goes round and a voluntary collection for the present. Comments like

HEATHER: Dear Grant. All the very best with your future endeavours. I know you'll be a success. Love, Heather. Kiss. Kiss.

TABITHA: All the very best for your next steps and life post-here. Tabitha.

NINA: Grant. You're right to leave. This place is full of fucking snakes. Best wishes. Nina.

DIM: Mate, this place won't be the same without you. I'm going to miss you heaps. Love you long time, tiger. Dim. Fat smooch on the lips.

CHORUS: Around 3 p.m. on that last afternoon the preparations begin. Bowls of crisps—salt and vinegar and plain, occasionally chicken—

Salada crackers.

Safeway cabana.

Bega cubes.

Perhaps a packet of Tim Tams?

Warm juice.

The phones are turned on to answering machine.

And then the speeches…

TABITHA: Nina? Would you care to do the honours?

NINA: No.

TABITHA: You've been Grant's team leader for a long time.

NINA: You're the fucking boss, yes?

Beat.

HEATHER: [*to* NINA] Have some cabana, love.

TABITHA: Right. Grant's been with the department for… twenty years, is it? I wasn't here when Grant started—none of us were actually. Grant has been our longest serving staff member—after Sammy. No I wasn't here but I have seen photos of a fresh-faced and bushy-tailed 21-year-old Grant. And he looked quite the charmer. Like a young Joseph Cotten.

Polite laughter.

He certainly didn't look like he had any idea what he was getting himself in for.

Polite laughter.

HEATHER: This place has ruined him.

Polite laughter.

TABITHA: Grant has seen a lot of changes take place here. The restructures, the development of a central administrative database, our services going online. I'm sure there are many yarns he could tell.

DIM: Give him a quart of whiskey and he'll sing like a canary!

Polite laughter.

TABITHA: I couldn't begin to detail the immense contribution he's made to this place in that time. Grant, you've been a very valued colleague and friend to all of us here. You've been…

She looks away from GRANT.

This place will be poorer for you not being in it. We will miss your humour and friendship. You have to promise to stop by sometimes. Don't forget us completely. We'd like to see how you're getting on. Well… a good speech is a short one so…

She raises her glass of juice.

Everyone follows suit.

TABITHA *and* GRANT *stare at each other.*

We wish you all the very best. Primary Industries is very lucky to have you. To Grant.

EVERYONE: To Grant.

Everyone drinks.

GRANT *is still staring at* TABITHA. *He comes to.*

GRANT: What can I say? I've spent half my life in this place. I won't know what to do with myself Monday morning.

Polite laughter.

I could tell you some stories about some of the characters from this place over the years. But perhaps we'll save that for drinks later. I don't want to lower the decorum of this event.

Polite laughter.

GRANT *tries not to cry.*

I just… I just wanted to say that some of the best people, best friends I've ever met came out of this place. And while I'm not unknown to complain—

DIM: That's the truth!

Polite laughter.

GRANT: I'm not going to remember the grumbling so much or the things I didn't like but all the things, all the people that I did.

GRANT *can't speak. He's trying very hard to keep it together.*

Everyone looks at each other, slightly awkward. No-one knows what to do.

HEATHER *holds up her juice.*

HEATHER: To Grant.

Everyone holds up their juice.

EVERYONE: To Grant.

TABITHA: And now for something a little different. Trevor has been keeping a secret from us.

DIM: He's got crabs!

Stifled laughter.

TABITHA: No. Thank you, Dim. He's actually a singer. And he would like very much to farewell Grant with a song. So, everyone, let's hear a warm, encouraging and non-judgmental applause for Trevor!

Everyone applauds.

TREVOR *steps forward.*

He has gone to some effort for this performance and is dressed a tad Duran Duran.

TREVOR: Some of you have commented on how I've changed these last few months.

DIM: You've waxed and your jeans are tighter.

Stifled laughter.

TREVOR: And it's because we lost a dear colleague a little while ago. And it made me think about dying and how you don't get to choose when it happens or how it happens. And how terribly short life is and so you have to… you have to get out of bed and get on with it. I think we forget that sometimes.

HEATHER: Well said, Trevor.

EVERYONE: Here here.

TREVOR: This is for Grant for being brave, for taking a chance and making a change.

TREVOR *sings 'Leaving on a Jet Plane' by John Denver.*

During the song, each team member says goodbye to GRANT *and returns to their cubicle.*

When TABITHA *hugs* GRANT *goodbye—he does not let her go.*

TABITHA *extricates herself from* GRANT*'s embrace and walks away without looking at him.*

DIM *winks at* TABITHA *and she smiles back at him.* GRANT *watches on, devastated.*

GRANT *looks around the DDDPTS.*

Phones ring, the printer prints, the sounds of the office.

The lights fade to darkness as GRANT *leaves the office for the last time.*

THE END